SAS
at the

July–November 1916

The War Diaries of ASR 'Old Bill' Ransley

EDITED BY SHONA WILKIE

DayOne

ISBN 978-1-84625-542-7

British Library Cataloguing in Publication Data available

All Scripture quotations, unless stated otherwise,
are from the anglicized edition of the English Standard Version
copyright © 2002 Collins, part of HarperCollins*Publishers*

Joint publication with SASRA and Day One

Day One Publications
Ryelands Road, Leominster, HR6 8NZ, England
Tel 01568 613 740   Fax 01568 611 473
North America Toll Free 888 329 6630
email sales@dayone.co.uk
web www.dayone.co.uk

SASRA
Havelock House, Barrack Road, Aldershot, Hants GU11 3NP
Tel 01252 310033   Fax 03000 302 303
Email admin@sasra.org.uk
web www.sasra.org.uk

Printed and bound in Great Britain by TJ International Ltd

The Battle of the Somme

Somme.
The whole history of the world
cannot contain a more ghastly word.

Friedrich Steinbrecher

The Battle of the Somme is etched in Britain's memory for more than being a blood bath. It was the first major offensive of World War 1 in which British troops did not play a supporting role but a leading one, with British Commander-in-Chief Sir Haig and the battle's British Commander, Sir Henry Rawlinson, planning the strategy. Because of its scale, it required the deployment of a mass-citizen army. This meant that almost every British family had a member on the front line, resulting in the whole of Britain feeling the pain, struggles and loss of each stage of battle. It was an intense five months, with sometimes two battles running consecutively and a total of ninety attacks.

July, 1916	August, 1916	September, 1916	October, 1916	November, 1916	December, 1916
			▶ Battle of the Ancre Heights		
▶ Battle of Bazentin Ridge		▶ Battle of Thiepval Ridge			
▶ Battle of Ginchy		▶ Battle of Guillemont ▶ Battle of Transloy Ridges			
▶ Battle of Delville Wood		▶ Battle of Morval	▶ Battle of the Ancre (2)		
▶ Battle of Albert ▶ Battle of Pozières Ridge		▶ Battle of Flers-Courcelette	▶ Battle of the Ancre		

On 1 July 1916 the front line stretched fourteen miles from Montauban to Gommecourt, and every stage of the offensive and attempt to move forward saw heavy casualties and varied outcomes. If the advancement of the front were pencilled on a map, it would look like the

steps to a salsa: a few steps forward followed by a few steps back, repeated over and over again. The Allies had advanced a mere six miles by the end of the Battle of the Somme on 18 November 1916, at huge human cost on both sides.

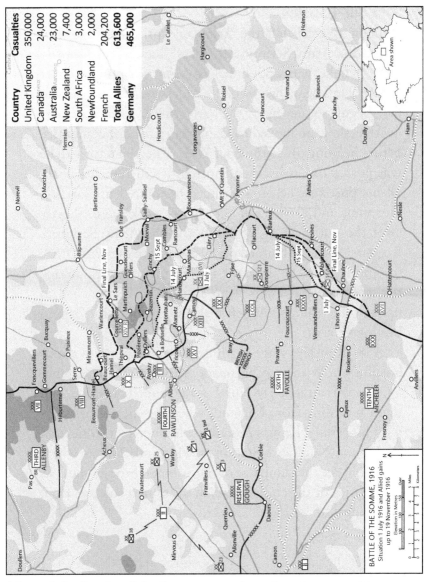

Country	Casualties
United Kingdom	350,000
Canada	24,000
Australia	23,000
New Zealand	7,400
South Africa	3,000
Newfoundland	2,000
French	204,200
Total Allies	**613,600**
Germany	**465,000**

BATTLE OF THE SOMME, 1916
Situation 1 July 1916 and Allied gains
up to 19 November 1916

Map of the Battle of the Somme, 1916. Wikimedia CC0 Public Domain

'Old Bill' Ransley

William Ransley left the Army in April 1889. He then joined the Army Scripture Readers' Society, and shortly after that he was appointed as Army Scripture Reader (ASR). He began his work in Aldershot, where he had first begun soldiering in the early 1880s. After ten years in Aldershot, he moved to Canterbury for a few months, before heading off to the Boer War. When he returned, he was posted to Dover, then Shortcliffe and Winchester. In all his postings, he often visited the injured in Garrison Hospitals and carried out a lot of his work there. Shortly after the outbreak of World War I the Army Scripture Readers' Society obtained permission from the War Office to send Readers to the front to do spiritual work among the troops. No Readers were allowed to be attached to units at the front, so ASR Ransley was sent to the base in Boulogne in 1914.

ASR Ransley worked tirelessly among the various hospitals in Wimereux throughout the war. In December 1915 he was attached to Number 14 General Hospital, and upon returning from England, where he spent Christmas with his family, he was posted to Number 5 Convalescent Camp and Number 8 Stationary Hospital. This is where he would see the slaughter of the Somme through the eyes and stories of the endless stream of injured soldiers from both sides.

A.S.R. Ransley, 1914

Image from original diary © SASRA

I had lunched and said goodbye to my wife and three girls and started off to the Railway Station. The platform was crowded with Officers and soldiers going to the Front. Here I met one of my brother Readers, Mr Gordon Howard, late Rifle Brigade, with whom I was to travel. Punctually at 1 p.m. the train started and passed through Kent. Only when Folkestone was reached was the silence of this company broken. The soldiers went straight on-board the Channel Passenger Steamers awaiting them. We were all soon on-board. We moved at 3.05 p.m. I took one look over the ship's side towards the receding shore of dear old England. We had left behind us our common everyday life of peaceful times and begun to realize that we had entered upon our share in the stern business of War. We reached Boulogne at 4.30 p.m. Reader Worbey introduced Mr Howard and myself to the Bishop. He allotted us our respective sphere of work, mine being Wimereux, a sea-side resort situated about three miles north of Boulogne. My work was to be entirely in the hospitals.

The War Diaries of ASR 'Old Bill' Ransley

July 1916

A wounded man told me: 'Different men act differently under shell-fire—some cry, some swear, some pray, and some go mad.'

Medical

Staff of No.8 Stationary Hospital, 1917.

Image from original diary © SASRA

Each General Hospital could have as many as two hundred orderlies working there. These were troops from the Royal Army Medical Corps, one of the British Army's specialist corps whose role was to work alongside the Medical Officers to provide medical services.

I visited 19 wounded German Prisoners, giving each of them a German New Testament.

I made a special effort amongst the Hospital Orderlies by visiting them in their huts and inviting them to a Voluntary Service; for I had felt that perhaps the Personnel had been neglected. I explained that I would hold an informal Service at any hour of their own choice, as they had told me that they

Military

A Corporal of Horse (CoH) of the Life Guards proudly displays his medals.

Military

The British Army ranks

Private
Lance Corporal
Corporal
Sergeant
Staff Sergeant
Warrant Officer
Second Lieutenant
Lieutenant
Captain
Major
Lieutenant Colonel
Brigadier
Major General
Lieutenant General
General
Field Marshal

did not care for a strictly C. of E. Service, or for the inconvenient hour of 6 p.m. at which that Service was held; and that their Chaplain wanted to meet them in this way.

They decided 8.15 p.m. as their most suitable time. Accordingly, I was there with one of their number, who had volunteered to play the organ. Only 8 attended, [comprising] 1 Staff Sergeant, four Sergeants, and 3 Privates, the Sergeants only attending, as they told me afterwards, 'to hear "Old Bill" (myself) preach'. On the seven following Sundays, I persevered with them, by visiting them and inviting them to the Service; but only the organist turned up. So I gave up this special Service, and helped the Chaplain at his 6 o'c one.

It is the remarkable testimony of many who have been responsible for conducting Voluntary

Medical

Wounded German prisoners being placed in an ambulance for transportation to a Base hospital. July 1916.

© *Imperial War Museums (Q124)*

There were two types of Base hospitals: General and Stationary. Stationary Hospitals could hold up to four hundred patients and General Hospitals could hold up to a thousand. There were around one hundred General and Stationary hospitals in the Somme area during WWI, some run by the British Army, some by the Canadian Army and others by the Australian Army. These were usually set up in large pre-war buildings, such as hotels.

Services in our various Base hospitals that Doctors and Orderlies are very difficult to get to attend them. I am disposed to think that the explanation as regards the Orderlies at our Base hospitals is, they have comfortable beds, good feeding, regular Pay days, and town attractions. These conditions tend to foster self-satisfaction and the spirit of indifference towards spiritual things. Then, of course, there is the 'fear of man that bringeth a snare', which accounts partly for their attitude. Many would not only like to attend Services, but to be wholly on the side of God; but until a man, living the corporate life of the Army, has taken a definite and open stand for Christ, he is very rarely found courageous enough to ignore the jeer & chaff of his comrades, who, more often than not, conclude that if a man attends a religious service or meeting he is necessarily professing to be religious, and treat him accordingly. 'Halloa! you've been to the Scripture Reader's Tent' or 'to Church!' is often said to men [who are] returning from these places, and is sufficient to 'choke them off' in too many cases, when there is not the softening influence of suffering, which our sick and wounded go through, to counteract this 'fear of man' and indifference, as suffering certainly does counteract it, as shown by the eagerness with which the patients ask for Services, and like to be talked to upon the subject of religion.

Large convoys of wounded arrive daily, and are evacuated the same day. All speak of 'heavy casualties'.

Cultural

Two British soldiers enjoying a drink of rum near the Chalk Pit, Pozières, 1916. They are standing on a pile of elephant iron, used for dug-outs and emplacements.

© *Imperial War Museums (Q 4619)*

During the Battle of the Somme a gallon of rum was distributed between sixty-four men. They received a ration of approximately a third of a pint over a week. It was initially distributed to fight the cold and damp of the trenches but rations were quickly more widely distributed: to men who undertook burials but also to give 'Dutch Courage' to those going 'over the top'.

A wounded man, elderly, godly, and a Sunday School teacher, told me: 'I am sorry the authorities give an issue of Rum to our Boys before going "over the top". I noticed two of my Regt too intoxicated to get over the enemy's trenches in our attack. Either they were not used to Rum, or they had drunk more than their proper share which was issued before our advance.'

Another wounded man told me: 'Our Divisional Commander told us before the attack, that this time we could expect to carry the enemy's position without suffering many casualties. But as we walked (we were ordered to walk) forward to the attack in the open, we were mowed down by their Machine guns until our advance was completely stopped and before reaching our objective.'

Military

Men of the Machine Gun Corps in action with a Vickers machine gun (left) and captured German MG 08 machine gun, Moquet Farm, September 1916.
© Imperial War Museums (Q 1420)

Machine guns had been used for years before WW1 but they were improved by 1914 and able to fire 600 rounds per minute. They were, however, very clunky and difficult to manoeuvre, particularly when trailing through muddy terrain. It could take up to four men to work one. The German Army used them particularly powerfully in 1916, causing thousands of injuries and deaths.

I visited 50-odd wounded German Prisoners, and gave each a German New Testament.

Wounded arriving and leaving all day. The whole of the Staff worn out with the work of it all.

About 200 wounded German Prisoners arrived in a deplorable condition—dirty, smelling, and most of them with very bad wounds of every description: bayonet, bomb, shrapnel, shell and bullet wounds. Sixteen of them had limbs amputated in the evening. Many had frightfully disfigured faces.

All the wounded very uncomfortable owing to the intense heat, and the Nurses and Orderlies very fagged, but working heroically—they are simply magnificent! It is marvellous how quickly the wounded are dealt with during these awful 'Rushes', as they are usually referred to. Speaking of these 'Rushes' (Convoys, one after another, rushed in and out in the one day), a Sergt remarked: 'I suppose we are not the only people having "rushes", in a time like this; I suppose they have big rushes in Heaven, too.'

Another 16 amputations, and 3 deaths among the Germans.

Our 29 Wards and 12 Marquees crowded with wounded! I wrote short letters for patients all afternoon and evening. Distributed Gospels and Lavender bags: the latter were very acceptable. The suffering and consequent moans and groans of the wounded while their wounds are being dressed is very distressing.

A wounded Sergt told me: 'Just before I was wounded I saw our stretcher-bearers bring four

French women out of the German first line of dug-outs which we had taken. I had heard of this sort of thing before, but this was the first time I had seen it.'

The telephone continually in use to-day with messages as follows: 'Are the German wounded all right?' 'See that they are well cared for.' 'Do not allow any unkind treatment.' 'Are the German wounded quite comfortable yet?' 'Are they getting everything they need?' 'Have you enough beds for them? If not, clear our own men who are slightly wounded out to Con. Camp, and occupy their beds!'

Seventeen wounded Germans were paraded and put in a Motor which was to convey them to the Railway Station. They missed the train owing to delay in starting from the Hospital, caused by the nurses in their anxiety to insure that all of them were well supplied with cigarettes and chocolates.

I saw our slightly wounded being sent to Con. Camp to make room for Germans, and our 'Sitting' patients, like the 17 Germans just referred to, are hobbling along from their different wards to the Motors. 'Now then those men, come along, hurry up, don't be all day!' is shouted to them. These had not been in hospital more than 8 hours; the 17 Germans had been in 3 weeks.

84 'Sitting' cases of German wounded rather unexpectedly arrived. Our own Patients in the Convalescent section of the Hospital, who a few days before had occupied Marquees and had been put into new huts owing to the severity of the weather, were moved back to the Marquees so that

the Germans might occupy the huts. In the huts the Germans had spring beds and mattresses with three blankets, while our men in the Marquees had to sleep on boards with three blankets and no mattresses. It was suggested that our men be given an extra blanket, as the weather was frosty, and many of the Patients had a temperature of 102. The extra blanket was refused, with the remark: 'The men are not put into the Convalescent Camp to be pampered and made soft, but to be hardened for duty at the Front again.'

A special Concert was being given for our wounded in one of the Wards (not too large a place).

Cultural

Group of the No.5 Convalescent Camp Concert Party-
"The Whiz-Bangs" - 1916.

Special concert.
Image from original diary © SASRA

Medical

1. Grand Hotel, Wimereux,W.View.
(14Stationary-Interic-Hospital)
Burnt in 1916.
2. Victoria Hotel, Wimereux
(14General Hospital - Infection),
& Grand Hotel,S.W. View.

1.Golf Hotel,2 miles N.of Wimereux
(Australian Voluntary Hospital).
2. Chateau Mauriciene, Wimereux
(Section "Rawal Pindi" Hospital)

14 General Hospital

Images from original diary
© SASRA

14 General Hospital was located in Wimereux in what was once a hotel (Hotel Splendide). It was extended in June 1916 to include Château-Mauricien.

It was suggested that a percentage of 'the poor Germans' should be admitted to the concert. Strange to say, the request was *not* granted!

A German Major, a wounded Prisoner of War in our Hospital, was walking past one of the sentries placed over them to guard them, without his Red armlet on, which he should have been wearing, and said to him in English: 'Why don't you salute me, how dare you ignore a Prussian Officer!' The sentry, an old soldier, replied: 'You go and put your armlet on, and quickly, or I, a British Private, will put you in my sentry-box!' The Major was furious

Military

Medal created and awarded by the British Government in 1854.
Wikimedia CC0 Public Domain

A Distinguished Conduct Medal (DCM) was a decoration for gallantry for non-commissioned soldiers, first given out in 1854. During WWI, 25,000 DCMs were awarded to men and women.

and went and reported him to the Commanding Officer. Another surprise: the sentry's authority was upheld!

A patient said to me: 'What! Still here? You visited me 14 months ago in the 14 General Hospital. Old Fritz has given me another "packet" (wound) to get on with.'

A re-enlisted Sergt, badly wounded a second time, showed me a photograph of his wife and girls; also a letter from a Salvation Army Captain in America. He said: 'I adopted him when an orphan and brought him up. He is a splendid lad and he loves us all very much, and we are all proud of him.' I wrote a letter for him to his wife. After he had left for England, I learnt from one of the Nursing Sisters that he had been awarded the DCM in this war, and that in the fight in which he was last wounded, he had distinguished himself and been recommended for the VC. Yet he had not spoken a word to me about it, and the sister only learnt it from the Doctor.

Military

Private Henry Green 10562. Unit: 8th Battalion, Royal Fusiliers. Death: 7 October 1916, Somme, Western Front. Commemorated on the Thiepval Memorial.
© Imperial War Museums
(HU 93422)

ASR Nick Wilson, Tidworth, England.
© SASRA

The 8th and 9th Fusiliers were part of the 36th Brigade within the 12th (Eastern) Division, an infantry division. Fusiliers served with notable distinction in WWI and the Battle of the Somme. In 1968, the Royal Fusiliers amalgamated with the Royal Northumberland Fusiliers, the Royal Warwickshire Fusiliers and the Lancashire Fusiliers to form the Royal Regiment of Fusiliers, who are now based in three locations. One of these is Tidworth, where our Army Scripture Reader Nick Wilson is currently bringing the gospel to the men and women there.

Ten more Germans died from wounds during the night.

Several intelligent wounded men of the 8th and 9th R. Fusiliers told me of our men coming under our own Artillery fire, or barrage, and of having to retire from positions won, owing to our Reserves not coming up in time, with many casualties as a consequence.

I talked with a wounded Guardsman who knew Reader Johnson. He spoke well of his work at Mons, and in the Barracks at Windsor before the War.

A re-enlisted man, badly wounded, said to me: 'Our Officer, an Insurance Agent in Civil life, is a rotter, and I am glad he got a hole through him!' I said: 'Can you not sympathize with him now, knowing as you do what suffering is—you are now both in the same boat.' 'No, because he is the most selfish man, and the biggest Bully I have ever met. He and three Officers lived in a dug-out with 3 blankets each, and when bread was issued they always had 5 loaves between them, leaving only 2 loaves to share out amongst the whole Platoon, so we used to toss up to see which Section should have 2 loaves; the remainder had the biscuits. He knew nothing about his Job, and was always bullying those who did. Not a man in the Platoon respected him, and like myself, they were glad to see him "get it". And if I ever meet him in Civil life, I'll give him a good hiding.' You can imagine how difficult it is to get a talk about spiritual things with a man when in such a mood as he was then in! However, he turned the subject, and told me about the fight in which he got wounded, and said: 'It would have done your heart good, as an old soldier, to see the magnificent way our Division crossed the open ground to the attack in skirmishing order under the murderous fire of the Bosch! The New Army are game boys.'

Military

Canadian troops just out of the line after the Battle of Courcelette, during the Battle of the Somme, pose with trophies on an Autocar UF21 30cwt lorry, September 1916.

© *Imperial War Museums (CO 827)*

The Canadians were heavily involved in WWI and the Battle of the Somme was no exception. In July, the Royal Newfoundland Regiment was the first to step in but they suffered heavy casualties with fewer than 10 per cent of their 800 soldiers surviving the offensive. During the duration of the Battle of the Somme 24,000 Canadians lost their lives.

A wounded Canadian said to me: 'An English Tommy who had spent 12 months at the Front in France, and came home to England wounded, told me before I came out: "You need not want to go out there, it is a perfect hell when a bombardment is on!" I replied to him: "You are safe out of it anyway, and I suppose I stand the same chance as you!" In my mind I thought he was exaggerating, and he certainly did not change my desire to go out. Well, I have been up at the Somme, and I never want to go through such an experience again. I found it very much worse than anything the man in England had described to me! The fact is, it is impossible to realize what advancing to an attack in a modern bombardment is until one has actually been through it. I shall never attempt to dissuade a man from coming out. It is best that he should remain ignorant of what he is in for, and come out, as we all do, in the highest of spirits. If one tells the facts as I was told them, like myself, "they wouldn't believe it", as the song says.' I then got my word in, and told him about the Queen of Sheba's testimony and that she came to prove King Solomon with hard questions: 'It is a true report … and the half was not told me.' He was really interested in my talk.

An Australian, 44 years old, very badly wounded in the shoulder, told me that he had never been in a sick-bed in his life before. And I can quite believe him; for he was so restless and fretful, and would keep moving about, and he groused tremendously. I suggested to him that it would be best for his wound

Biblical

Piero della Francesca, Legend of the True Cross—The Queen of Sheba Meeting with Solomon.

Now when the queen of Sheba heard of the fame of Solomon concerning the name of the LORD, she came to test him with hard questions. She came to Jerusalem with a very great retinue, with camels bearing spices and very much gold and precious stones. And when she came to Solomon, she told him all that was on her mind. And Solomon answered all her questions; there was nothing hidden from the king that he could not explain to her. And when the queen of Sheba had seen all the wisdom of Solomon, the house that he had built, the food of his table, the seating of his officials, and the attendance of his servants, their clothing, his cupbearers, and his burnt offerings that he offered at the house of the LORD, there was no more breath in her.

And she said to the king, 'The report was true that I heard in my own land of your words and of your wisdom, but I did not believe the reports until I came and my own eyes had seen it. And behold, the half was not told me. Your wisdom and prosperity surpass the report that I heard. Happy are your men! Happy are your servants, who continually stand before you and hear your wisdom! Blessed be the LORD your God, who has delighted in you and set you on the throne of Israel! Because the LORD loved Israel for ever, he has made you king, that you may execute justice and righteousness' (1 Kings 10:1–9).

if he tried to exercise a little self-control and try to keep still. He looked up at me with a stare of undisguised astonishment at my unreasonableness, and burst out: 'Good God Almighty, He never made me to be knocked and slashed about with iron and steel—my body was never meant to be a receptacle for old Krupps rubbish!' He said it so seriously, it seemed to me the more comical.

A young soldier hit in the chest asked me to read and pray with him, which I did, and often times after.

A Canadian, slightly wounded, and marked to be sent to a Con. Camp, said to me: 'I wish I had got a "Blighty" one.' I told him of many who had wished like him, and were sorry that they got what they wished for. Then he began to swear and grumble about everything and everybody. The contrast between patients who were badly wounded, or are sick and very ill, and those who are not, is remarkable! The former are patient, uncomplaining, and most grateful for the least kindness shown to them; the latter, many of them, are shocking grumblers.

A patient made the following mixed statement to me: 'I am always kind of religious; I don't profess to be good, but I don't oppose religion.' So we talked of what it meant to be truly Christian. And he promised to try the real thing.

Wrote a letter for Sergt E—, 17 years' service, & in the War from the commencement without a day's sickness, but now wounded in the right arm. He told me his father was killed on board ship when it

Military

Australian troops marching to the trenches near Fricourt,
September 1916.

© *Imperial War Museums (Q 1560)*

The Australians' principal involvement at the Somme was
in the offensives leading to the capture of Pozières and
Mouquet Farm. They suffered a loss of 7,000 lives over a
month and a half, as well as 15,000 serious injuries.

was torpedoed; a brother was killed in Belgium; and
another brother was wounded in France.

A wounded Australian soldier, Dutchman by birth,
35 years old, and who had worked with Germans
before the War, and could speak their language,
told me: 'When we advanced we took no prisoners,
we killed every mother's-son of them, because we

had seen the Germans turn their Machine guns on our wounded, and club them with the butts of their rifles, and even throw up star shells at night to enable them to see our wounded to fire on them.'

During the month of July, 11,000 wounded passed through our Hospital.

August 1916

A badly wounded Australian said: 'When my Battalion went into the trenches for the first time, the Saxons shouted, "Go back to Australia, we only fight England." We shouted, "We've come a long way to fight you, and you have got to have it." Then they began to shout abuse at us, shouting: "You are a lot of curs, sons of convicts and sheep-stealers, and we'll wipe you out." Well, with their Machine guns they certainly played old Harry with us the first time we attacked them, and they kept it up to the last moment before our close approach to them with our bayonets threatened danger; then, they all threw up their hands and cried "Mercy Kamerade!" but we showed no mercy. If they had played the game and kept up the fight when we reached them, we would have shown mercy; but they will only fight while they feel safe behind Machine guns.'

The same Australian told me: 'I saw a brave German Officer in Gallipoli who came on leading his men, mostly Turks, with sword and revolver in hand, under a murderous fire from our troops, and a worse fire from our ships at sea. The Turks were falling by thousands, and yet this Officer kept

Military

Gallipoli historical centre.

The Gallipoli Campaign took place in Turkey between April 1915 and January 1916. The Allies were defeated by the Ottomans.

leading and yelling to his men. We admired his pluck, and shouted: "don't shoot at that hero, take him Prisoner, if possible!" But a few minutes later he was killed.'

A Sergt, badly wounded in the left leg and arm, expressed his delight at having me to talk to, and he began telling me about his mother, for whom he had a very great affection, and he showed me her photograph. Having accepted a New Testament from me, he volunteered the remark: 'I should like to be able to give my whole mind to the things of God.' So we talked about these things.

The next time I saw him, he was crying with pain, & apologized to me for not showing a braver spirit. Another patient in the ward had already expressed to me that afternoon his sympathy, saying: 'I'm sorry for that poor Sergt, he is going through it!' So you will understand that there was no need for the Sergeant's apology.

As I have already noted, it is not always easy to get a talk upon spiritual matters with some patients if they happen to be eager to tell of their battle experiences. On this occasion I was the first to show an interest in the Sergeant's experiences at the Front, and I purposely asked him to tell me how he got wounded. Then he told me the following story:

'I was on duty in the trenches. My Company Officer had just visited me to ascertain if everything was all right. Just after he left me, a German shell burst overhead; consequently, a Private, who was standing beside me, and I, at once dived into his dug-out. While there, another shell burst and knocked our earthworks to pieces, burying us

Medical

Dressing station near Ginchy, September 1916.
© *Imperial War Museums (Q 4257)*

Wounded British troops on a hospital train leaving for the base at Heilly, September 1916.
© *Imperial War Museums (Q 1258)*

The Field Ambulance set up Dressing Stations where the injured could be given basic treatment to get them into a good enough condition to travel to a Clearing Station. From there they either returned to the front or were sent by train to a hospital for further treatment.

together under the debris. In trying to get free I found I was able to move my right arm a little, and I worked it until I got it entirely free, and then, having cleared the dirt out of my mouth, which was nearly chocking me, I shouted to the Pte, to know how he fared. I gathered from his reply that he was not hurt much, and that he could move his limbs. So we arranged to help each other to try and free ourselves by pushing with our bodies. This pushing process went on with a certain amount of

Medical

Battles of the Somme. Bringing in the wounded. Stretcher-bearers carrying man on stretcher, near Carnoy and La Boisselle, 2nd July, 1916.
© Imperial War Museums (Q 65412)

Close to the front line were units where a Medical Officer, some orderlies and trained stretcher-bearers operated. The Field Ambulance trained the stretcher-bearers to evacuate the injured from the trenches. This was a very risky role because of the danger of getting caught in the firing line.

success until it became more than I could bear, so I called to the Pte to stop pushing, and told him I was sure that my leg was seriously hurt. It was night, & very dark, and there was nothing that we could do

Biblical

Bible.

You will not fear the terror of the night, nor the arrow that flies by day, nor the pestilence that stalks in darkness, nor the destruction that wastes at noonday.

A thousand may fall at your side, ten thousand at your right hand, but it will not come near you.

You will only look with your eyes and see the recompense of the wicked.

Because you have made the LORD your dwelling place—the Most High, who is my refuge—no evil shall be allowed to befall you, no plague come near your tent. For he will command his angels concerning you to guard you in all your ways.

(Psalm 91:5–11)

but wait in hope of help coming to us. That help came in the persons of our Colonel and one of his Majors who were passing by. I cried to them for help without knowing who they were, and when they realized our predicament they started to dig us out, one digging while the other held an electric torch; this they did in turns, and found it difficult and delicate work to avoid unnecessarily hurting us. When I was clear, my leg was found to be badly smashed and my rifle embedded in my thigh by the weight of a beam and some sandbags which had fallen on top of me. Men were fetched to take us away, which they did in waterproof sheets, suspended by means of ropes tied to the corners. In this way these *brave* fellows carried us under cover through the communicating trenches, themselves walking along the top of the parapet, thus exposing themselves to the enemy's fire. Needless to say, this was awkward and difficult work for the bearers. When clear of the trenches we were placed on proper stretchers, and conveyed to a Dressing Station about 3½ miles away. Before arriving there I had become unconscious, and knew nothing more until I came back to consciousness in the train just before our arrival at Boulogne. I then found that my wounds had been dressed, and I was feeling fairly comfortable.

'I shall never be able to speak too highly of those two Officers, and the splendid Stretcher-bearers. Every Stretcher-bearer is a hero, and every wounded man would say the same of them.'

When he had finished his story, of which this is only a part, I looked at my watch, and said: 'I have been most interested. I fancy you have not been feeling so much pain during the last hour?' He smiled. Before I left him, I spoke to him from some verses of the 91st Psalm. He ultimately went to England.

I had given a young sick patient a Lavender bag with the text, 'He careth for you', tied on it, and remarked to him: 'I'm sure you must have proved the truth of that text at some time in your experience.' 'Yes,' he replied, 'it is quite true that He cares for us, and I know it,' and then very sadly, he added: 'but I don't think of these things in the way I used to. I was once a Sunday School Teacher, and while such I committed a wrong which led me to resign, and since then I have not attended Services, and have been very unhappy, and the more I try not to think about it, the more I have to. Do not think I mean that I have been a notorious evil liver.' Then he told me the following story:

'The Vicar had appointed me Secretary of the Sunday School Outing Committee, and as such I was responsible for the sale of Tickets, etc., connected with the Outing. I was engaged

Medical

Lavender.

Lavender was used as an antiseptic but also as a way to distract patients from the foul stench of infected wounds. It was said to lift their spirits and calm their nerves. Voluntary organizations and medical staff would hand out lavender bags to increase patients' comfort.

to one of the Teachers, and I gave her and her two lady friends a ticket each, intending to pay for them myself, but afterwards I found I was unable to do so in time. When I realized my position, I made up my mind to own up to it to the Vicar and offer him my resignation. I confessed the whole thing to him. He accepted my resignation, and then harangued me, and even threatened me with prosecution. However, he didn't. Of course I left the Sunday School, also the Church, and ever since I have despised Clergymen and lived recklessly as regards these matters. But while at the Front I have thought much about the affair, and altogether I have been unhappy. I do not think the offence was a small one, but I do think the Vicar a brute in his way of dealing with it, after I had so frankly and seriously owned up to it.' We had a long talk about it, treating the incident as a by-gone as far as the Vicar was concerned. Before I left him, we prayed to God and settled up things with Him, and when he left for England, he told me: 'Everything is quite all right now: I forgive, and am forgiven, and I am quite happy, and when I get Home I will join a Church.'

A very young lad, sick, with whom I had a nice talk, told me that his grandfather, father, and 2 uncles were at the Front.

A Nurse asked me to try to get a short message from a badly wounded man who was dying to put in a letter to his wife, which she also suggested I should write. I had talked with the man several times before he became so ill. I endeavoured to get the desired message. A good deal that he had said was incoherent, but in some of his broken sentences I made him out to say: 'Tell her my message was peace' ... 'Only by God's help can I get better' ... 'She is the best in the world' ... 'I have a dear little girl' ... 'Two dear boys' ... 'This is a strange war' ... 'Jesus is a good Friend.' He made a sign to me to give him a piece of paper and pencil. I gave it [to] him (the Nurse was now by his side), and he tried to make a capital E; this he made backwards, and then dozed off. The Nurse laid him back from his sitting position, and we left him, the Nurse promising to arrange for the Matron to write to his wife. He died a few hours later.

I spoke to an elderly Scotchman, accidentally wounded, seriously, by the explosion of a bomb. He lost his left eye, and was wounded in one lung, right arm and wrist. He was very bright and cheerful. He told me he had been trained for the Mission Field, but had never taken up the work. He asked me for a copy of St John's Gospel, which I was able to give him. Then he told me in the presence of several Up-patients in the ward the following: 'My favourite text has always been Psalm 34:6—"This poor man cried, and the Lord heard him and saved him out of all his trouble." I have that text written in every book in my Library that I have at Home. I have proved the truth of those words in my present trouble more than ever before. And I advise you lads to make it your motto.' It was a splendid testimony, and very likely did more good than anything I might have said, coming from him under such circumstances.

I had a helpful talk with a wounded lad, an orphan, aged 25. He told me a good deal about his 'bad young life', as he called it. 'It all began,' he said, 'with bad companionship.'

September 1916

Rev. A—, the Chaplain attached to the Hospital at this time, always invited me to give the Address at one or two of the Services on Sundays, and on occasions when he had to conduct Services at other places, I have conducted the whole Service at his request. Other Chaplains have preferred to let the Service drop, under similar circumstances, if unable to procure another Chaplain, rather than ask a layman. At the close of one of the Services which I had been conducting for Rev. A—, a Regular Sergeant of the Rifle Brigade, who knew me in the

Military

A dump of empty 4.5-inch and 18-pounder shell cases, Fricourt, September 1916.
© *Imperial War Museums (Q 1471)*

Shells, or explosive projectiles, were used extensively by the British Army during the Battle of the Somme. It is estimated that 1.6 million shells were used to bombard the German front line in just seven days. These were the main cause of shell shock, a condition that baffled the medical personnel because of the psychological nature of the symptoms.

A star shell is a piece of artillery used to light up the battlefield when it was dark or as a means of signalling.

Rifle Depot in pre-war days, made himself known to me, and we had a delightful talk about old times. He told me: 'The two years' War experiences which I have gone through have made a difference in my life for the better, and I mean to attend to Religion.'

A lad said to me: 'I have read my New Testament which my mother gave me before I left Home, every day, and I regard it as my best friend that I have out here.'

A badly wounded lad, aged 19, asked me: 'Do you believe that a soldier goes to Heaven by virtue of his dying on the battle-field? Men often argue about it in the trenches; some profess to believe it, and others do not. I have heard Chaplains preach it. I for one cannot believe that if a man has not lived a holy life, his dying on the battle-field will save him, and though I am not able to explain exactly why I think so, I feel satisfied in my own mind that it cannot be so, and for this reason: when I lay wounded on "No man's land", as young as I am, horrible things in my past life came up before my mind, which made me feel afraid, and I prayed to God for forgiveness. For 36 hours I laid there in terror as the shells and star-shells burst over me, and I prayed as hard as I could to Jesus Christ. I thought of those arguments I have told you about, but I did not feel I could trust [that] the blood, which was slowly trickling from my wound, could atone for my past sins. Although I volunteered for the War, I don't mind telling you that I did not want to die in "No man's land", but wanted to live and go home and see my mother again. And in spite of that awful time in "No man's land", here I am, and I own that I owe it to God's goodness. And when God has heard and answered prayer, it is up to a chap to thank Him, and though I have not been religious before, I am going to try to serve Him for bringing me safely out of that Hell.' I regard this as a remarkable statement from one so young.

I assured him that he was right, and quoted several texts in support of what I said to him. As he belonged to the C. of E. I not only quoted Acts 4:12; John 14:6; but also the opening words of the Prayer of Consecration in the Communion Service: 'Almighty God, our Heavenly Father, who of thy tender mercy didst give thine only Son Jesus Christ to suffer death upon a cross for our redemption; who made there (by his one oblation of himself once offered) a *full*, *perfect*, and *sufficient* sacrifice, oblation and satisfaction, for the sins of the *whole* world.'

What the lad said he had heard Chaplains preach, I also heard preached by a C. of E. Chaplain in the

Many rooms.

And there is salvation in no one else, for there is no other name under heaven given among men by which we must be saved. (Acts 4:12)

In my Father's house are many rooms. If it were not so, would I have told you that I go to prepare a place for you? (John 14:2)

Churches

English Church at Wimereux.
Image from original diary © SASRA

English Church at Wimereux. I made a note of his words at the time, which were as follows: 'We may be sure that every one who has laid down his life at the Front for his Country, did so willingly and definitely as a sacrifice to God and we may believe that their sacrifice is accepted by God for righteousness. Indeed, God needed their help in this way.' Then followed an inconsistent and illogical argument in support of his plea for our prayers for these very men who had fallen in battle—men, he had just before assured us, who had had their sacrifice accounted to them for righteousness, and this, too, from a Minister who, I suppose, had used the words in the Prayer of Consecration thousands of times!

Talking with a young wounded soldier to whom I had offered a New Testament, he volunteered the statement to me: 'I belong to the YMCA religion.' It reminded me of the Sergeant's wife, who said to me when I visited her in her quarters in pre-war days: 'I belong to the Ritualistic religion.'

To-day, I found myself in the awkward position of having to try and defend the YMCA which was being attacked by a cynic, who remarked to me in the presence of 15 up-patients. Unfortunately, he was only voicing what I had heard many others say at different times. Not that I accept their verdict, for I am fully aware from my own experience in similar work on Salisbury Plain and other places, when I have been in charge of Refreshment Bars, how certain men will grumble and complain unjustly, and misconstrue our conduct in the most suspicious and uncharitable way. This particular man said: 'In the next war I shall join the YMCA—that is the kind of army to be in. I like their patronizing way

Organizations

Exterior of a YMCA hut
at No. 5 Convalescent Camp at Cayeux.
© *Imperial War Museums (Q 5409)*

The Young Men's Christian Association first went out to France in November 1914 and established recreation centres around the main Army bases. They provided snacks and hot drinks to troops.

when a soldier goes into their Huts—"We welcome you good, brave young fellows who are so gallantly fighting for us. When we think of all that you go through for us we feel it a great honour to do what we can for you. We hope you will use the Hut and the free note paper, etc." It comes well from those who are not older than myself, and who are as fit in health as myself for soldiering; but because they happen to wear a "White choker" (Clerical collar) they are exempt. And then as to their supplying us with cheap refreshments, they do no such thing, but fleece us by charging us 1d a cup for tea, so-called, but really it is spoilt water, and less than half a pint at that. It is the YM Commercial Association they should be called, not Christian Association.' This grouse caught on, and others began. One said to me: 'I bought a packet of "Woodbines" at a YMCA and when I went to use them I found a little ticket in the packet marked "for our wounded".'[1] I asked both these men if what they had told me was fact, or whether they were making it up? When they assured me it had been their experience, I told the man who complained about the Cigarettes that he should see the Hut Leader about it, as he might be absolutely innocent of such packets being in his stock. He did so, and it was found to be a mistake, and of course it was rectified. After a long talk about these matters, some of them admitted the usefulness and benefit of the Association.

---

1 Packets labelled 'for our wounded' were to be distributed free to wounded soldiers in hospitals, not sold to non-wounded soldiers.

A wounded man accepted a New Testament from me, and said: 'The Stretcher-bearer that carried me off the field told me: "It is a remarkable fact, that of the hundreds I have carried off the field there has not been one but had a New Testament or Bible upon him."'

A wounded Canadian, Roman Catholic, had a lengthy conversation with me, in course of which he deplored the perpetual quarrel between RCs and Protestants, and especially was he distressed about the Rebellion in Dublin. 'As Britishers,' he said, 'we ought all to live in unity as we do at the Front: there we respect each other, and live and work together independent of Creeds.'

A young Australian with fractured femur, and who had been in Egypt, asked me if I knew Abysiah outside Cairo? I seized the opportunity of telling him it was there, when aged 19, and a Private soldier, I knelt by my bedcot to say my prayers for the first time since I was a boy, in a large barrack-room with 150 men in it at the time. Then he asked me about the difficulties of living the Christian life in the Army. He was most interested and thanked me for the talk.

An elderly man, wounded in the head, said to me: 'As bad as my wound is, and the consequent suffering, I do really thank God for it; for it has been the means of leading me to think seriously, and by God's grace I am a changed man.' He died very shortly after the visit.

There have always been a great number of 'SI' (Self-inflicted) cases pass through our Hospital. As many as 40 were admitted in one week. These cases are classified under A, B & C. 'A' includes those who are found guilty of *purposely* maiming themselves; 'B' those who are found guilty of *negligence*; and 'C', those who are found guilty 'without negligence', but through some inexcusable fault. I never met one who admitted his guilt. Certainly, some are innocent; but unfortunately, witnesses who might have been able to testify to the fact, have been killed before the prisoner has been brought to trial, in which cases, they are usually placed under category 'C'. None seem to get the benefit of the doubt.

Military

Men of the 10th Battalion, East Yorkshire Regiment (Hull Commercials) marching to the trenches.
Wikimedia CC0 Public Domain

In the hope of being sent home from the front line, some soldiers would inflict a wound on themselves, usually a shot. This was considered a capital offence, although all 3,894 soldiers found guilty of this crime in WW1 were sentenced to imprisonment rather than death.

Many patients have told me that Conscripts are often sent out with only a month's training. One man told me: 'A certain Regiment which had a large number of Conscripts in its ranks had many "SI"s. On one occasion, some men of this Regt were running along a communicating trench and ran into the Adjutant and Sergt-Major. The Adjt asked: "What is the matter?"; "Our men are retiring on our left flank," they answered. "Sergt-Major, throw a bomb at them," commanded the Adjutant. The S-Major picked up a bomb and ordered the men back, and then inspected the whole trench. He found everything normal, and that no attack had been made, or retirement ordered.

A young wounded soldier asked me for a copy of St Matthew's Gospel. 'When a boy, at the request of my mother, I learnt that Gospel bit by bit until I knew the whole of it,' he said.

A young sick patient from the Front was very profuse in his thanks to me for my visit. He told me that he and a younger brother were 'Dean's Scholars' at Llandaff. 'As a Chorister,' he said, 'I used to get very sick of having to go to Church 3 and 5 times a day; but what I have gone through since I enlisted, especially out here, has made me long for those once unappreciated privileges.'

October 1916

A Scotchman, RA, wounded in the head, told me that he had had two brothers, older than himself, killed in the War—one at Mons, and the other at

Military

SEPTEMBER 25, 1925.

TEN YEARS AGO TO-DAY.

THE BATTLE OF LOOS.

SO NEAR SUCCESS.

Ten years ago to-day opened the battle of Loos, the greatest which the British Army had fought up to that date. In it a total of 250,000 British troops with 900 guns was engaged. The object was to break through the German front in Artois, where it was strongest, and re-cover Lille, while the French broke through the German front further east, in Champagne.

The terrain across which the British advanced has since the war recovered its old aspect. A desolate moor dotted with ruined mine-heads, damaged mining villages, and great slag heaps, across which ran the German front line of trenches—a veritable maze of works, provided with deep dug-outs and with steel and con-crete machine-gun shelters. The British, in fact, were to assault a first-rate fortress.

The assault was delivered with the most magnificent gallantry. For the first time large numbers of troops of the new armies raised in 1914 were employed in offensive operations.

The British went forward with such dash and determination in the face of a terrific fire that they broke very deeply into the German front. If reinforcements had been available and on the spot, an immense victory was in sight. But the reinforcements never came. The Germans recovered from their shock and rushed up reserves; and when next day fresh British divisions were thrown into the battle it was too late.

The net result was that a small salient was driven into the German front with prodigious suffering and loss. The Brit-ish casualties in the first three days of the battle (which did not close until the middle of October 1915) were 47,000 and were probably considerably in excess of the German losses, though 26 guns and 3,000 unwounded prisoners were taken by the British. But there was this to be said, that the new British troops had proved their signal value and that the heroism displayed by them and by the other British units has rarely been sur-

Newspaper clipping from 1925, found in ASR Ransley's original diary.

The Battle of Mons (Belgium) took place in August 1914 and the Battle of Loos (Belgium) in September 1915.

Loos. The news of the one killed at Mons caused his mother, aged 56, to go totally blind. His father who served through the Afghan War, was also serving in this war.

I had an interesting talk with a Sergt F—, Hairdresser by profession, and a Salvation Army worker. He was in a Look-out trench when a German shell burst and knocked the parapet on top of him, partially burying him, besides wounding him in the head. A lad of his Regt, less than 17 years old, dug him out. He gladly accepted a New Testament from me to replace the one he had lost at the Front. He told me some of his spiritual experiences in the trenches during 18 months. The following is particularly interesting, as coming from a Salvation Army worker: 'Recently, while in a communicating trench, passing ammunition along to the front—to the German's second trench which our men had just taken—a Roman Catholic Chaplain came along and asked if any of his men were there. The RC men at once declared themselves, as they always do, then the Chaplain asked them to say a Prayer, sentence by sentence, after him, which they did. The Chaplain continued his course along the whole line of the trench, repeating the same thing, many Protestants joining in, including myself. The men talked a good deal about the incident afterwards, and expressed a very high opinion of the Chaplain.'

I was talking to a few slightly wounded patients who were out of bed, when an elderly man, who had been several years in S. Africa and 7 years in Canada, said to me: 'I notice you are an old soldier, and you must know a lot of the tricks of the Service; can

Military

Left -Mr Hinde Page 353 343.
Centre-Mr Flemming
Right -Mr Ransley
Estcourt, Natal, S.A.War,
1899.

Image from original diary.
© SASRA

The Second Anglo-Boer War took place between October 1899 and May 1902. ASR Ransley served as Scripture Reader during this war before returning home and eventually going to France.

you tell me how I can get to "Blighty"? I don't want to eat Cordite, like a chap I know, it affects the heart too badly; the dodge of "picking up paper" is too old and well known. Can't you tell me a successful dodge?' 'Well,' I replied, 'I do claim to be an old soldier and to know just one more trick than a monkey, but I'm afraid I cannot tell you of one that would get you to "Blighty", unless it is this: join my branch of the Service—the Army Scripture Readers' Society. I have been to "Blighty" three times on leave since I came out in 1914.' The patients laughed, and said: that's the stuff to give 'em! Then the man said: 'The Army Scripture Readers' Society!—Is that your "Crush"? that's the "Mob" I'll join in the next war.' Then I told them of the wounded man who said to me: 'Some men long for a "Blighty one" (wound) to get them to England; I've got one that's going to be the means of getting me to Heaven,' and explained to them what he meant.

I came across a big Irishman in one of the wards, limping with a big stick; he was a re-enlisted man and elderly. I said to him: 'You have been wounded in the foot?' He replied in a brogue as Irish as could be: 'No, Sor, I met wid an accident—I fell into a hole and sprained my ankle.' I remarked: 'We have a lot of men come down from the Front injured in that way.' He evidently thought I was a Padre, and said: 'I beg your Reverence's pardon, I'd be ashamed, so I would, to deceive you, I'd be the last man in Ireland to do the like of that. I'll just tell you the God's truth. I met wid my accident through taking a drop too much—and that's what might happen to any man—and I was so drunk, I fell into a hole somewhere, I don't know where, for I was not after knowing rightly at the time the way things was.' I said: 'You ought to be a teetotaller!' 'That's what I'm after thinking myself; but a small drop wouldn't be no harm to me now in hospital, if so be the Doctor didn't object.' I asked him if he had ever heard of the Bill the Irish Veterinary Surgeon sent in for Professional attendance: 'To curing your Honour's horse till it died.'

I had begun to speak to Sergt G—, a Territorial, 30 years old, when he at once informed me that he was going to have his leg amputated that afternoon as it was impossible to save it. He gripped my arm, saying as he did so: 'excuse me taking hold of you, the fact is I am neurotic, and it helps me when I grip something. I have had two operations on this leg, and I suppose it has unnerved me, although I am not really afraid of the operation that is coming off this afternoon.' As he held me, I told him how I had been helped just before going through a serious operation by some verses at the end of the 91st Psalm. I read the last 3 verses from the Society's New Testament which I had given him, and which has that one Psalm in it. Then he opened his mind to me and told me how he had failed to live the life he knew he ought to have lived, and asked my advice, adding, 'I have never confided in any one before, so please do not tell anybody.' When I left his bedside, he put out his hand for me to shake, and as I held it, he said: 'God bless you and your noble work.' Before I left the ward, sometime later, he sent the Orderly to me to ask me to go to him again, which I did. He said to me: 'I am sorry to trouble you, but I want to thank you for what you have done for me, and to ask you to come again; and if you think it would help your work any, you are quite at liberty to tell my story.'

In the same ward there was a young lad, badly wounded, who had been there 9 weeks, and with whom I had many chats. The Nurse, this afternoon, asked me to read some letters of his which had come from England overnight, but which she had not time to read to him. There were four, and when I had read them, he became very bright and began to talk and laugh about the writer of one of them who had been a school fellow of his, and who in his long letter referred to their boyish escapades. At his request I answered three of them; his old school

Cultural

Organ and hymn books.

'Just As I Am' is a hymn written by Charlotte Elliott in 1835.

Just as I am, without one plea,
But that thy blood was shed for me,
And that thou bidst me come to thee,
O Lamb of God, I come, I come.
(...)
Just as I am, though tossed about
With many a conflict, many a doubt,
Fightings and fears within, without,
O Lamb of God, I come, I come.

fellow's I was to answer the next day. In each of the three which I wrote, he wished me to say that he hoped to be in England soon. Having finished the letters, I gave him a card with the hymn 'Just as I am', and a prayer on it. When he had read it he said: 'I like that hymn.'

Next day I visited the ward again. I found Sergt G— much better and brighter, as so many [are] after the amputation of a limb with which they have previously suffered so much in the endeavour to save it. I was about to begin to write a letter for him, when a Nurse came to me and whispered: 'You might go to F— (the lad whose letters I read to him the day before); he is dying.' The Sergt heard, and said: 'Yes, do go to the boy, never mind about my letter.' I succeeded in getting F— to recognize me, and then quoted, 'The Blood of Jesus Christ cleanseth from all sin', a text which I so often used with effect on the Battle field in the S. African War. He opened his eyes and repeated the words 'Blood … Jesus' five or six times, and then cried out in pain: 'I want to die, I've had enough of pain, I'm tired of it!' Then he motioned to me to give him a drink. He drank a few drops while I held him up, and when I laid him back again, he coughed, and asked me for a handkerchief. I gave him mine, it being the easiest to find, and he kept it. The Nurse came to him at this moment and spoke to him. He closed his eyes and became quite quiet, and I left him. When I returned to the Sergeant to write his letter for him, I found the C. of E. Chaplain was doing it for him.

I next spoke to an elderly man of the Royal Naval Division. He was sitting up eating his tea, and seemed to be enjoying a hearty meal. He said to me: 'My father has the Zulu medal like you are wearing, and he was in the Indian Mutiny, too, and is still "going strong".' We exchanged a few remarks about it and then I gave him one of the cards with 'Just as I am' on it, which I so often found useful for giving away. As it was past my tea-time and I had promised Sergeant G— I would visit him the next day, I just pointed out one of the verses on the card to the Blue-jacket, and promised I would talk to him about it on the morrow. 'So do, mate,' he said; 'I don't mind a talk about religion.'

As I was leaving the ward, another patient, J—, of the 1 East Surrey's and a Regular with 9 years' service, beckoned to me. I went to him, and he said: 'I heard you say you will be coming again tomorrow; will you speak to me when you come?' I of course promised I would.

According to promise, I visited the ward the next day to speak to Sergeant G—, the Blue-jacket, and J—, but imagine my surprise when J— said to me on entering the ward: 'Three died in this ward last night, including the Naval chap!' The other two were Sergeant G—, and the young lad that I spoke to about 'The Blood of Jesus Christ cleanseth from all sin'. The fact made my opportunity with J— all the more solemn, and we had a serious talk as arranged. I found that he had come from India with his Regiment to France, and excepting five days' leave, he has been at the Front nearly two years.

As a Regimental bomber he was cleaning bombs, when one exploded and blew off his left leg, broke his right arm, wounded his left hand, necessitating amputating his little finger, and wounded him in the stomach. He suffered awful pain, and said: 'I feel sometimes I would rather die than go through much more of this. It is only for the sake of Mother and Father that I try to bear it and live.' He told me that both his parents were Godly people, and to show that they were so, he handed me a letter of his father's to read. Then we talked about his own soul's salvation with the result he decided to live for God. After I had prayed with him, he asked: 'Would it be right to pray to God to take away pain?' 'Certainly,' I said, and then and there prayed for this. Immediately I had finished the prayer, he asked: 'Will he do it?' For a moment I hesitated, and an illustration came to my mind, which I gave him as my answer. I said to him: 'A table that is too weak to bear the weight that is upon it, must either be strengthened to bear the weight, or the weight must be taken off it—God will either take away the pain, or give you strength to bear it, as He did in answer to our Saviour's prayer in the Garden of Gethsemane—His will was done, which was to strengthen Jesus by the sending to Him an Angel. Jesus was submissive, and quite content that His will should be in line with His Father's will.' Afterwards I wrote two letters for him.

In the same ward, that afternoon, a Canadian and an Australian listened very sympathetically and with interest while I talked to them of the love

Organizations

A Salvation Army night shelter.

Wikimedia CC0 Public Domain

The Salvation Army sent 241 men and women overseas during WWI, with its main focus on France not starting until 1917.

of God. They were both badly wounded. The Australian spoke very warmly in praise of the Salvation Army and their work in Australia, and told me that he had a sister [who was] an Officer in it. These two men, like many other Colonials I have talked to during the war, have volunteered statements to this effect: 'Though I am nominally a Churchman, I prefer Chapel—the Church don't seem to "take on" amongst us out there.' Some C. of E. Chaplains, too, have told me that they have had the same thing said to them by Colonials. Of course I met some keen Churchmen, too, amongst the Colonials.

Next day, I saw J— again. He welcomed me with a smile, and said: 'I had no pain all night, and enjoyed some sleep, and oh, it was so sweet!' He told me that he trusted God for the pardon of his sins. For the next three weeks he suffered much pain, and he seemed near to death's door. Several times he quite lost heart and was rebellious. Under these circumstances I could only read him some few words from the Book, and pray, and on each occasion he became calmer and more hopeful. His mother and sister came from England to visit him. The visit was magical in its effect. He afterwards wonderfully improved, and ultimately went to England. On one occasion when he was downhearted, I told him of a couple of remarkable answers to prayer which I had recently experienced in connection with two men I was interested in, and I promised him that a few of us, who were accustomed to pray together, would pray for him to get better and be sent to England by Christmas. I was with him on Christmas Eve, and he said: 'It doesn't look much like being home for Christmas.' I confess I had my doubts about it being any longer possible. However, that very day, a sudden order came for an evacuation to England, and he was one of the number that went. When I said good bye to him, I reminded him of answered prayer, which I had told him about previously, including our prayers about himself. His face brightened up, and he said: 'I do believe God answers prayer; but it is hard to trust when suffering such awful pain!'

The prayers referred to above are two, both worth mentioning. My late Batman of No. 5 Convalescent Camp had been very ill. He was only a youngster of 20, and had been out from England 17 months at the Front without any leave. He had been sent to his Base after his discharge from hospital and wrote [to] me that he was 'expecting to "go up with the best of luck" again' (a phrase the Doctors use when sending men up to the Front). 'I can hardly stand,' he wrote; 'if I must go up like this, I will trust in God and hope for the best.' I ventured a bold reply; I said: 'Charlie, I know how hard it is to do one's duty at the Front when feeling so weak and ill. I have no access or influence with MOs to help you, but I am going to pray God three times a day that He will dispose the authorities to send you Home for a rest, and then you will be able, please God, to come out fit to do your duty.' I carried this out. About a fortnight after, I received a letter from him written in a London hospital. So prayer was answered, and he went to England instead of the Front. He came out to France again in the Spring of 1917, and was killed on November 27th. In his last letter to me (his 61st in the 17 months since he left me at No. 5 Con. Camp), dated November 3rd, 1917, he wrote: 'We are not "fed up" ... we are looking forward confidently to a satisfactory victory ... I am still smiling and persevering.' I had strongly advised him to take promotion, and I am glad to say that in a short time he became a Corporal.

The other case concerns a Private B—, RAMC. He started to serve God at the Front in the end of 1915, after he was wounded. Later he was transferred to a Unit in this district, and was one who used to attend my meetings in No. 5 Con. Camp, and after the break-up of that camp, he used to visit me in my Bell tent in No. 8 Stationary Hospital, where we usually had prayer together. One night he brought a comrade with him for instruction in the way of salvation, which proved helpful to the man he brought. Two nights after, B— came to my tent by himself to see me about his own spiritual state, telling me that what I had said to his comrade about making restitution as a part of a true repentance, had 'hit him up'. Then he told me a long story, which I cannot detail here; suffice it to say, it related to a serious military offence, the confession of which would possibly involve him and his wife and child. If punished, it might be imprisonment for him, and would affect him (and his wife indirectly) financially. I gave him my advice, and we prayed about it. About a week after, he came to me and said: 'Will you take care of this bag of coppers; they are English; I have been given them in change when spending French money since I

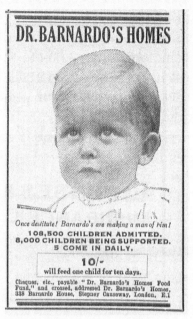
A 1931 advertisement for Dr Barnardo's Homes.
Wikimedia CC0 Public Domain

When Thomas Barnardo died in 1905, the charitable organization he had founded provided residential care to children across almost one hundred homes. Some children who lived there recall happy times and a sense of home, while others remember it as a difficult and lonely time. WW1 left many children orphaned.

have been converted, and I have been saving them up for Dr Barnodo's [*sic*] home as a thank offering to God for saving my soul, and bringing me safely through with my wound. There are £2 worth. Tomorrow, I am going to the CO and confess all. If I get imprisonment, you will be good enough to send this money to Dr Barnodo's [*sic*] for me.' I further advised him, and told him to be sure and explain, briefly and humbly, his motive for confessing his crime to the CO He did so, and found all concerned very sympathetic. The CO told him to carry on, that in the meanwhile the whole affair would be referred to the proper authorities in England. The news soon spread, and some of his comrades ridiculed him, saying in effect: 'Well, B—, you must be a fool! What about your wife and child, etc.' To them, he merely replied: 'God, who has brought me out of battles, and healed my wound, and better still, saved my soul, cares for my wife and child more than I can. He knows why I have done what I have, and I am quite content to leave them and the whole matter to Him.' Three others, who would be the first to own they were not religious, came to him and shook hands, and said: 'B—, old man, I admire your pluck, it's more than I could do,' and wished him well. This good will expressed by these three, more than compensated him for all the other ridicule which he had to meet. We now agreed to pray three times a day that the authorities might be disposed to let him off. I felt justified in this praying; for he had not evaded his obligation to answer his Country's Call, but paid his fare from Canada to come to

England and joined his first Regiment; obviously he could not join the other two from which he had deserted, [but] he had served faithfully and loyally at the Front and had been wounded. Now that he had owned up to his crime, not with the desire to escape the arduous duties of campaigning, by going to prison, as some have been known to do, but for conscience' sake, I was inclined to believe he had a reasonable chance of being let off by the authorities during a war like this, in which he had behaved well. I certainly believed that if he were to receive punishment, it would be very much less than he would get had he not given himself up as he did, and after the war found out and taken. During the enquiry into the matter, he was not without his temptations to doubt, especially on one day, when some men said to him: 'B—, what about your leave now? I see you have been passed over: no going to "Blighty" for you now!' This was a sore temptation, for he longed to go home as he had not been for over 12 months. Every man out there simply lives for his leave to go home. However, he resisted the temptation, and firmly trusted Him to whom he had committed the affair.

Some weeks passed, when he came to my tent with such a beaming face! He said: 'I paraded before the CO this morning, and he told me: "B—, your affair has been settled: you are let off, and you will hear nothing more about it."' I don't think there could have been a happier man in France than he was that night. Shortly after, he was given his Leave, which he had just missed. On his return, he was placed in [a] responsible position by his CO. So genuine 'Out-and-Out' Christianity does pay!

November 1916

I offered a young Canadian, who appeared to be a well-educated man, a N. Testament. He said: 'Thank you, I have one, and wouldn't be without it for the world! A chum of mine had one which he kept in his left-hand pocket, a German bullet struck it and passed through it, and dropped to the bottom of the pocket. I had heard of such happenings before, but I can vouch for this.' I asked him if he regarded

Cultural

A hobbit hole from The Lord of the Rings.

Trench fever is an illness caused by bites from lice. The bite causes a fever that lasts five days and severe headaches as well as muscle ache. It is said that J. R. R. Tolkien suffered from trench fever during the Battle of the Somme and wrote significant parts of *The Hobbit*, inspired by the horrors of war around him, while recovering in Birmingham Hospital.

the book as a sort of charm? 'Oh, no, I read the book regularly, as I have seen many others do in the trenches. And I am convinced that thousands of men who are going through this war are going to be better men for their experience in it.'

An elderly man of the Royal Engineers (New Army), in hospital with 'Trench fever', said to me in the hearing of several other patients, who were listening to our conversation: 'Do you really believe it is possible for a soldier to live the Christian life up at the Front, considering all they have to put up with there?' I answered: 'On your showing, you have done your duties there *without* the principles of Christianity and found it hard; try it *with* these principles in your heart, and you will find with others that it is possible and much easier.' I also explained how I had served God, by His grace, in the Army and through Campaigns. In the end, he was well satisfied with my arguments, and said: 'I suppose it is so if we are willing.' That same night, I was writing to a friend of mine at the Front—a Company-Sergeant-Major, who had 17 wounds which he had received in this war, and some of them dangerous ones, and who was out for his third time, voluntarily. He is a godly man. In my letter I mentioned the RE's query, and asked him for his opinion. I received the following reply, and read it in the course of an Address which I gave at a Sunday morning's Church Service in Hospital: 'In reply to the RE's query—I answer from several weeks' experience in the "hottest shop" on the whole front—*YES!* A thousand times, Yes!! It's not a hindrance as many would try to make out, but a great, wonderful, and invaluable AID!!'

A Territorial spoke to me rather enthusiastically on Church matters, and seemed to have a considerable amount of knowledge on the subject. He was particularly hot in defence of the much-maligned Clergy, especially those engaged in Missionary work abroad. I was the more surprised, therefore, when he followed his defence—a defence I readily backed him up in—by declaring his disbelief in the wisdom of Foreign Missions. 'In my opinion,' he said, 'it had the effect of making the heathen crafty, thieving, etc.' The patients around, listening, looked to me for a reply. I told them of a conversation I had had with an intelligent Fingoe, who was a Christian Catechist in S. Africa, which went to show that a *genuinely* converted person, whether white or black, dropped vices and lived virtuously: that the Fingoe had told me that the mischief in S. Africa was the same as we had at home—the contentment, too common, with mere nominal membership of the Churches. And I pointed out that Britain was once heathen and the good that is now in the nation was due to the practice of Gospel teaching by those who were real and true Christians. The whole conversation was so interesting to the men that they asked me to come another day to have a talk about these things.

Another Territorial of the R. Scots, to whom I offered a N. Testament, said: 'My sister gave me a Bible to bring out here, but I thought it too good an edition to use on Active Service, so I left it at

Military

ASR David Murray,
Edinburgh, Scotland.
© SASRA

*Troops of the
9th Battalion,
Royal Scots,
marching in wet
weather. Amiens–
Albert road,
September 1916.*
© Imperial War
Museums (Q 4263)

All six Royal Scots New Army Battalions were a part of the Somme offensive, from the very first horrific day in July 1916 through to the Battle of Arras. The Royal Scots Regiment merged in 2006 with other regiments to form the current Royal Regiment of Scotland. They are based in Pennicuik, part of the City of Edinburgh Garrison. Army Scripture Reader David Murray currently brings the gospel to the men and women across the Garrison's various locations (including Edinburgh Castle and Redford Barracks).

home, and I have been without one, so I will gladly accept yours and promise to read it.' Then he told me of his experience concerning the use made of Testaments by the men in the Column which took part in the Duke of Westminster's Expedition in Egypt, in which he was a signaller, and he assured me that his story was no exaggeration. He said: 'In that short expedition there was no Cigarette issue to the troops, but an issue of tobacco in tins. As the men had no pipes and no cigarette papers, they used the leaves out of their N. Testaments, and would make two cigarettes with one leaf. It was common to see a man tear a leaf in two pieces and give one half to a comrade, as half a leaf was just the right size for one cigarette. This practice was pretty general throughout the Column, and the men named the cigarettes "the New Testament Brand".' He also told me that on one occasion a Chaplain was passing through their lines, and noticing the men making these cigarettes, said to them: 'I told you, boys, you would find your Testaments useful.'

A Roman Catholic with his left eye out and his right arm badly wounded, asked me to write a letter for him to his parents, and also asked me for a N. Testament.

I had an interesting talk with a South African about religion, which led him to introduce the subject of the 'Black and White' difficulty, and he declared his belief that the Missionaries increased the difficulties. His was the usual worldly-wise theory over again.

A lad only 17 years old, who had one of his arms blown off in the fighting on the Ancre, was very gay and jubilant in relating how our men had paid Fritz out in the fight. He said nothing about his pain or how he lost his limb until I asked.

A young Scotchman with a fractured femur, caused by a sniper, showed me a letter which he had received from his father, forwarded from the Front, so that his father at the time of writing did not know of his lad's wound. In the letter he wrote: 'Never fail to play the man although you are far away from home!' He told me he had always tried to do so, and that his experience at the front had made him determined to be much better in the future. 'I have not found it so difficult to keep straight in my Regiment as I was led to expect I should.'

One of the KSLI, 20 years old, and 12 months at the front, said to me: 'I have never forgotten the parting words of an old gentleman spoken to me at Eastbourne: "Always go forth to all your duties in the strength of the Lord God Almighty." In every fight and charge that I have been in, I have remembered his words, and they have given me courage.'

A Sergeant of a Swansea Battn, married with four children, and a Baptist, thanked me for my visit and asked me to come again. 'I joined,' he said, 'at the beginning of the war on the conviction that it was my Christian duty. I said to my wife, "I am going to France to do my bit to help keep the Germans from coming over here to treat you and our children, and others, in the way they have treated the Belgians." I think that our people—even our soldiers—at this stage of the war, do not remember as they ought, what the enemy did to women and children at the beginning, and are still doing.'

Military

ASR Lee Philipson,
Winchester,
England.
© SASRA

Trenches.

The King's Shropshire Light Infantry was made up of twelve battalions in 1916, seven of which were involved in the Battle of the Somme. In 1948, the KSLI became known as the Light Infantry Brigade and in 1968, after amalgamating with a number of regiments, it became the Light Infantry which, after further amalgamating with four other regiments in 2007, formed what we know today as the Rifles. The five Regular and two Reserve battalions are located across the UK and Germany in eight locations, including Paderborn, where ASR Ray Hendricks is located; Winchester, where ASR Lee Philipson carries out his ministry; Edinburgh, where ASR David Murray shares the gospel; Lisburn, where ASR Paul Somerville visits the men and women posted there; and Aldershot, where SASRA's HQ is located.

A young Territorial, living a Christian life, according to his own statement, and a great admirer and advocate of the YMCA, very thoughtlessly, and I think, ignorantly, said to me: 'I think most men in the army at the front will be different men, spiritually, in consequence of the experiences they are passing through up there, especially am I hopeful it will be so, *because the men are different to the men of the old army*—the men in the army today, unlike those of the army in pre-war days, have not enlisted because they were *hungry or in disgrace*; they are *educated*, and are *guided by principle*, etc.' Needless to say, I rated him. But after all, he only expressed what many others think, and some others say. In my presence, a group of Sergeants were discussing 'No. 1 Field Punishment', and denouncing it as degrading. In course of their arguments, one said: 'In drawing up a code of punishment for *this* war, the authorities should have taken into account the *class* of men *now* composing the Army. In the old days, for instance, when flogging was in vogue, the men composing the army of those days were not *capable of feeling degradation* in the way *our* men are to-day!' I at once chimed in, and told him that, '39 years ago, I saw an old soldier jump out of his bed and go up to a young soldier of the "Short-Service" system, who had recently come into the room, and pull his ear for using a filthy expression, which I have heard you, and many others of your so-called superior class (which he claimed to be in the army today), use more freely than I had ever heard it used before the war.' And after [my] explaining matters as they appeared to me, he was really sorry he had expressed himself as he had, and to his credit, he apologized.

Regimental-Sergeant-Major, 1/Wilts, operated upon for Appendicitis, told me: 'The most distressing thing I have witnessed at the front (he had been in everything from the commencement of the war) was our wounded men caught in the barbed wire in "No man's land", and left hanging on it to linger and ultimately die in view of both the enemy and ourselves, without our being able to rescue them. Some I have known to hang there as long as 8 days. Their cry for water is terrible!' ... 'Occasionally, men have voluntarily gone out to try and bring them in, only to be killed in their attempt. Usually, permission to try and bring them in is refused for this very obvious reason. Often times the poor chaps receive other hits while hanging there.' He also corroborated what others have told me: that the Germans will purposely fire at them, and when successful in hitting them, would send up a cheer with fiendish glee.

L/Corporal I—, East Lancs., 19 years old, asked [me] to pray with him. He told me that he had believed in prayer since a child. 'My mother,' he said, 'brought me up to believe in prayer, and I have always practised it, and know its power and worth.' He had gone through a terrible experience since he was wounded. He was hit with an explosive bullet, and was four whole days and nights in 'No man's land' before help came to him. During this time he subsisted on just the water which he had in his water-bottle; his 'Iron', or 'Emergency', rations he was unable to eat owing to his sore mouth and swollen tongue. 'I prayed during those four days,' he told me, 'until I became utterly exhausted. If it is not irreverent to say so, I think I had a faint experience in prayer of what Our Saviour went through in the Garden of Gethsemane.' While with us, his left leg was amputated, and his mother came out from England to visit him, which, humanly

Olive tree.

Biblical

Then Jesus went with them to a place called Gethsemane, and he said to his disciples, 'Sit here, while I go over there and pray' ... Then he said to them, 'My soul is very sorrowful, even to death; remain here, and watch with me' (Matthew 26:36, 38).

speaking, saved his life, as has often been the case in similar instances: the mother's and wife's influence being so tremendously effective in the joy which their presence gives to the patient. His is one of the many cases which exemplifies the marvellous endurance of man under extreme suffering.

A Company-Sergeant-Major wrote [to] me from the front of an experience he had had in September, 1915: 'This day,' he wrote, 'I went "over the top". It was about 2.30 p.m. and I was going round collecting the remnant of my company, and I came across a Sergeant whom I knew in the 9th Battalion K. R. Rifles, and who had since joined the 17th with me. He was looking very white and shaken and I stopped and I had a chat to him for a few moments. He had heard about my being buried, and asked me about it, so, of course, I told him. "Well, Topper," he said, "I used to *laugh* at Religion! But after what I

Military

An aerial photograph of Schwaben Redoubt.
Wikimedia CCo Public Domain

The Schwaben Redoubt was a network of German trenches and was one of the Germans' key defensive locations during the Battle of the Somme.

have seen today, and what you have told me, I begin to think there's something in it! Any way, I shan't laugh at it again!" Unfortunately, the poor chap was badly wounded in the "Schwaben Redoubt", and last week it came through that he had "died from wounds". I wonder—I should very much like to know—whether or not he accepted Christ before he died, or whether he died still thinking only that "there was something to it!"'

End of 1916: The end of the Battle but not the end of the War.

May the year of 1917 see the end of the horrible War!

ASR Ransley

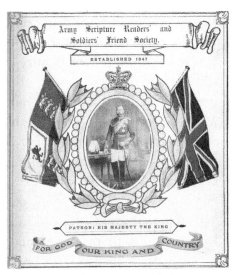

Image from original diary.
© SASRA

The ministry of SASRA since 1838—and today

Old Bill's ministry is in many ways no different from the ministry of SASRA today. Still now, SASRA Scripture Readers encounter soldiers and airmen where they are and seek to meet their spiritual needs by bringing them the gospel. Each year across British military bases they offer hundreds of New Testaments, 90 per cent of which are accepted. SASRA continues to hold fast to the amazing truth that God's living Word changes lives and saves souls. Since 1838, in times of peace and in times of war, Scripture Readers have had the great privilege of sharing the Good News of Jesus Christ with our military personnel.

The exact early origins of SASRA are unclear, though it is said that in the early 19th century a group of officers prayed for an association to come into being. There followed a series of events and people, all contributing to the beginnings of SASRA. One of the most influential men in this was Sergeant Rudd, who saw an opportunity to meet the spiritual needs of serving personnel and began offering Bibles and literature to those around him in Woolwich in 1816. At first he was reprimanded, even threatened, but some years after these incidents, in God's grace, the King's Regulations of 1825 officially authorized Bibles and Prayer Books to be distributed to all who wanted them—at public expense! This eventually led to the Chaplain General, supported by Christian Officers, appointing Christian ex-servicemen to read Scripture to soldiers, and later airmen, in their barrack rooms. This was the beginning of SASRA and its Scripture Readers as we know them today.

ASR Ransley met men and women who faced struggles of all kinds, and, in their physical, mental and spiritual pain, he brought them the hope and the joy of the Good News. Our Scripture Readers do just that today, meeting men and women of the British Armed Forces, engaging with them where they are, and sharing with them the hope they can find in Jesus Christ. What a privilege to be able to do this under royal patronage and with an MoD Charter!

The number of Scripture Readers working for SASRA has fluctuated over the decades, and today, with a dozen Readers, we are eager to expand the work significantly in order to reach more men and women of the military with the gospel. In the current global and political climate, this is urgent kingdom work as our men and women

Army
Scripture Reader
Ray Hendricks,
Paderborn,
Germany.

Army
Scripture Reader
Lee McDade,
Catterick,
England.

Air Force
Scripture Reader
Meg Atkinson,
Brize Norton,
England.

Images © SASRA

train and prepare to go in harm's way on our behalf. Our Scripture Readers enjoy a unique privilege of being able to go 'behind the wire', where the church cannot go. It is a large mission field, currently 117,000 men and women (excluding reserves), and we pray we will be able to send plenty of workers to the harvest. You can help us in our ministry and help the church fulfil her Great Commission through supporting SASRA in two vital ways: you can pray for the ministry and you can give to the ministry.

SASRA relies entirely on the generosity of Christian men and women and their free-will giving as well as their prayerful support. You can sign up to receive our prayer materials, our Magazine or your Regional Report via the website, where you can also make a one-off donation to the work or sign up to support us regularly. You can also access all of this via our Facebook page. These platforms will also keep you updated on the current work of SASRA, so please do visit the website and 'like' SASRA's Facebook page for more information.

Visit our website: www.sasra.org.uk

If you would like to make a gift, set up a standing order or receive information about making a gift in your will, please use the website address above or contact SASRA on 03000 301 302 and ask for the Finance Director.

Visit our Facebook page: facebook.com/sasra.org.uk

Yes I want to HELP PARTNER with SASRA's ministry.

☐ **A ONE-OFF GIFT**

☐ **£10 can buy a hard-wearing Bible for a soldier or airman.**

☐ **£50 can fund a Scripture Reader taking the gospel to soldiers/airmen on exercise.**

☐ **£100 can pay for a whole Bible study course.**

☐ **£ _____ (please fill in the amount of your choice)**
I enclose my (cash/cheque) donation to sponsor SASRA's work.

☐ **I do not wish to receive an acknowledgement.**

Or if you wish to donate using your credit/debit card please either visit the donate page on the SASRA website **www.sasra.org.uk** or alternatively telephone SASRA HQ on **03000 301302**

☐ **REGULAR GIFT to support the work of SASRA**

STANDING ORDER

To _____ Bank PLC _____ Branch _____ Sort Code

Please pay to the account of SASRA, sorting code 161926 account number 10139767 the sum of

£_____ ☐ each month ☐ quarter ☐ half year ☐ annually from my

account number ☐☐☐☐☐☐☐☐

Starting on ☐☐ / ☐☐ until further notice.

Signature: _____ Date: _____

Boost your donation by 25p of Gift Aid for every £1 you donate

Gift Aid is claimed by the charity from the tax you pay for the current tax year. Your address is needed to identify you as a current UK taxpayer. In order to Gift Aid your donation you must tick the box below.

☐ I want to Gift Aid my donation of £_____ and any donation I make in the future or have made in the past 4 years to the Soldiers' and Airmen's Scripture Readers Association.

I am a UK taxpayer and understand that if I pay less Income Tax and/or Capital Gains Tax than the amount of Gift Aid claimed on all my donations in that tax year it is my responsibility to pay any difference. I will notify SASRA if I wish to cancel this declaration, change my name or address or no longer pay sufficient tax on my income or capital gains.

Signature: _____ Date: _____

(PLEASE RETURN TO SASRA HQ)

Name Mr/Mrs/Ms/Other_____

Address _____

_____ Postcode: _____

Email _____

We will hold the information you give us for administrative purposes. If you do not wish to receive any further news from us please write to: Supporter Services at our address. We never pass on contact details to any other organisation.

SASRA Havelock House, Barrack Road, Aldershot, Hampshire GU11 3NP
Telephone: **03000 301302** email: **admin@sasra.org.uk**

www.sasra.org.uk

Registered Charity No 235708 In Scotland SCO 39130

Further titles in this series:

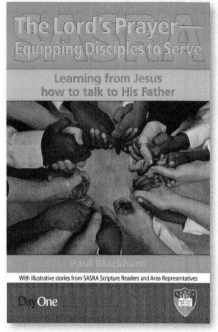

The Lord's Prayer—Equipping Disciples to Serve
PAUL BLACKHAM
With illustrative stories from SASRA Scripture Readers and
Area Representatives
ISBN 978-1-84625-559-5

*From the very front line that supports our armed forces personnel
comes this thriller of a book that, from the start, transports us
from the first and second heavens right into the third – and to the
very side of Jesus! I have never read a book like it before. Instantly
readable, we owe many of its luminous Scripture references to
my former colleague Dr Paul Blackham. These are interlaced with
short, punchy 'real-life' stories from anointed Scripture Readers. The
Lord's Prayer has been touched with a compelling reality for us all
in these wondrous pages.*

The Rev Richard Bewes OBE, writer and broadcaster;
former Rector of London's All Souls Church, Langham Place.

Scripture Reading to the End
ASR WILLIAM G RANSLEY
and his Gospel witness, France, 1918
Edited by Bill Newton
ISBN 978-1-84625-603-5

We are pleased to warmly commend SASRA's publication of "Scripture Reading to the End." In it he writes short descriptions about his experiences visiting and ministering to the sick and wounded soldiers serving on the "Western Front" during the first world war. Whether comforting and encouraging Christians to remain faithful and to keep trusting the Lord or in challenging those who didn't believe, his obvious love for Jesus and for the people he served is a refreshingly simple formula. He appears not to engage greatly in religious debate but to concentrate on reading the scriptures and talking about knowing and following Jesus as Saviour and Lord. We would do well to follow his example.

Graham Nicholls, Director of Affinity